Grandpa's Magic Memory Box

A Children's Book About Dementia

G.M. Grace

Copyright

First published by Global One Books LLC October 2023

Copyright © 2023 by Global One Books LLC

First edition

Dedication:

To my beloved grandson, Alex,

You are the bright star in our family's sky, a source of endless joy, and a reminder of the beauty in every moment. Your boundless Love, patience, and understanding have inspired me to share the story of your great-grandfather, Grandpa Jack, and his journey with dementia. May this book serve as a testament to the enduring power of family, Love, and resilience.

And to my dear father, Grandpa Jack,

You were the heart and soul of our family, and your unwavering strength and grace in the face of dementia touched us all. Though marked by challenges, your story is a testament to the profound Love and connection that transcends the boundaries of memory. This book is a tribute to you, a remarkable man who inspired us with your spirit.

With all my Love,

G.M. Grace

P.S. Alex wanted everyone reading his story to have one more coloring book than the one included at the end of his story. So, have a parent or someone older, scan this code to get it for you. You'll have to have a printer.

Alex loved weekends with Grandpa Jack. Together, under their favorite tree, Grandpa would share tales from the "olden days," and Alex would hang on to every word.

But one day, things began to change. Grandpa forgot where he kept his glasses and even the name of Alex's beloved toy lion, Leo.

"Grandpa Jack has something called dementia," Mom gently explained.

Dad added, "But he still loves you very much, even if he sometimes forgets names or stories.

"Think of a brain like a library," Dad said. "For Grandpa, sometimes the books get mixed up or are hard to find." Alex nodded, starting to understand.

It wasn't always easy.
Alex felt a storm of
emotions—sadness,
confusion, sometimes
even anger. But with
Love and talks, he
learned it was okay to
feel and share.

Dementia
Alzheimer's
Cancer
A

At school, Mrs. Robinson talked about families and the challenges some face. Alex found comfort in knowing some of his friends were on similar journeys.

Though Grandpa forgot at times, their bond never wavered. They found new joys—painting, singing, enjoying Strawberry shakes, and walking hand in hand in the garden.

While flipping through an old photo album, Alex discovers Grandpa was a pilot. "We can sketch your adventures together," Alex

exclaimed, drawing a plane with bright paints.

Grandpa's fingers may sometimes falter, but they remembered the strings of his old guitar. Together, they sang tunes from Grandpa's youth, filling the room with melodies.

The garden was Grandpa's living storybook. Each plant had a tale, and though they changed with each telling, the essence remained, teaching Alex about growth, life, and patience.

"Grandma's secret cookie recipe," Grandpa recalled. As they baked, the sweet aroma brought back memories, and they created new ones with every bite.

movie CINEMA

Walks with Grandpa became journeys to the past. Each building and each corner had a story. And Alex soaked in every tale, weaving them into their ever-growing tapestry of memories.

The duo took up projects - building birdhouses, crafting, and even trying out inventions. These moments, full of laughter and learning, became cherished memories for Alex.

Grandpa's stories under the stars were magical. "That's Orion," he would say. Even the universe, with its vastness, became an intimate space for sharing dreams and wonders.

Alex proudly introduced Grandpa to his friends. The playground was filled with laughter as Grandpa showed magic tricks and shared little pearls of wisdom.

Alex had an idea! "A Magic Dementia Memory Box," he declared. A special place for photos, mementos, and stories - a bridge to Grandpa's memories.

In the attic, amidst memories of yesteryears, they found the perfect box. "This held your Grandma's dancing shoes," Grandpa recalled with a smile. "A box of cherished memories, for more cherished memories."

HELLO

Painting strokes, sticky fingers, and bursts of laughter filled the room. "Every star you place, Alex, is a memory we've shared," said Grandpa, eyes gleaming with unshed tears. Alex beamed,

"And many more to come!"

HELLO
TICKET
TICKET

Every item in the box had a story. The model plane from their museum trip, the flower from their garden day. "And this," Alex said, placing his letter, "is my

promise. Whenever you forget, Grandpa, we'll open this box and remember together."

Things had changed, but one thing was clear: their bond was unbreakable. Alex knew that memories wrapped in Love were stronger than any illness.

Dear Caregivers and Parents,

Understanding dementia can be challenging, especially when explaining it to young minds. The journey with a loved one living with dementia may be filled with complexities. However, it is also an opportunity to teach children about compassion, patience, and the enduring power of Love.

With their innate curiosity and resilience, children can adapt and thrive even in difficult situations. However, they will often take cues from the adults around them. It is essential to approach the subject with openness, honesty, and reassurance. Emphasizing that while memories might fade, the Love and bond shared remain constant can be a comforting perspective.

Engage children in activities that help them connect with their loved ones. Whether crafting, listening to music, or simply spending time outdoors, shared experiences can foster understanding and create lasting memories.

Children will have questions that might not always be easy to answer. It is okay not to have all the answers. Providing a safe space to express their feelings, fears, and frustrations is important.

Lastly, always remember to take care of yourself. Caring for someone with dementia can be challenging, and self-care is crucial. By ensuring you are at your best, you are better equipped to support and guide the young ones in your care.

May this book serve as a gentle tool to initiate conversations, inspire understanding, and emphasize that while dementia might change certain aspects of a relationship, it does not define it.

With warmth and understanding,

G.M. Grace

Use this code to leave an Amazon review.

Bonus
Coloring Pages

On the last page of "Grandpa's Magic Memory Box," the story comes full circle as young Alex and Grandpa Jack sit together, a heartwarming lesson about the importance of understanding, compassion, and cherishing memories in their hearts.

Dear Readers,

In the heart of our special adventure with Grandpa Jack and Alex, we've learned something truly magical - the power of Love, understanding, and the treasure of memories.
As they sat side by side, Alex and Grandpa Jack couldn't help but smile. They knew that their journey had taught them important lessons about dementia and the enduring bond of family.

1. **Understanding Dementia**: Through their adventures, Alex had learned that dementia was like a puzzle. Sometimes, Grandpa Jack's memory was a little jumbled, but that didn't change the Love they shared. It was essential to be patient and understanding, just like Alex had been.
2. **Cherishing Memories**: The magic memory box had shown them that even when some memories faded, new ones were created. The box was a symbol of Love, a place to hold the moments they cherished together, old and new.
3. **The Power of Stories**: Sharing stories with Grandpa Jack had created a bridge between generations. It made him smile, even when he couldn't remember every detail. Stories had the power to connect people, and that connection was a gift.

So, dear friends, remember that every day is an opportunity to create beautiful memories with the ones you love. Just like Alex and Grandpa Jack, your Love and understanding can work wonders, even in the face of challenges.

With Love and memories that last forever, *Alex and Grandpa Jack*

Writing an Amazon review for our children's book on dementia is more than just sharing your thoughts—it's about sparking a movement. By taking a moment to pen your insights, you illuminate a path for countless other parents seeking guidance. This book strives to bridge a gap in children's literature, making the topic of dementia approachable for young readers. However, its impact is magnified when shared by genuine experiences like yours.

Your feedback not only aids other caregivers in their quest for the right resources but also shapes the future of such content. The author thrives on understanding your perspective, ensuring even more poignant resources emerge in the future. Moreover, your review can be a beacon, encouraging parents to broach tough conversations about mental health, and in doing so, build a more understanding and empathetic generation.

In an interconnected world where every voice counts, yours can be the one that makes all the difference. Dive into the narrative, share your story, and let's redefine how we approach dementia in children's literature together.

Please scan the QR code below to go directly to the review page. And, thank you from my heart.

MY GIFT TO YOU
SCAN ME!
FOR MORE COLORING PAGES